FACES IN A SINGLE TREE

Faces in a Single Tree
A Cycle of Monologues

ᵇ

BY ROBERT PACK

David R. Godine : Publisher
BOSTON

First published in 1984 by

DAVID R. GODINE, PUBLISHER, INC.
306 Dartmouth Street
Boston, Massachusetts 02116

Library of Congress Cataloging in Publication Data

Pack, Robert, 1929–
Faces in a single tree.
1. Monologues.   I. Title.
PS3566.A28 F3   1984   811'.54   83-49005
ISBN 0-87923-521-7
ISBN 0-87923-525-X (pbk.)

FIRST EDITION

Printed in the United States of America

ACKNOWLEDGMENTS

The author wishes to thank the editors of the following magazines, in which the poems appearing in this book were first published: *The Agni Review, Antaeus, The American Scholar, Black Warrior Review, The Chowder Review, The Denver Quarterly, The Georgia Review, The Gramercy Review, The Hudson Review, The Kenyon Review, The Massachusetts Review, The New England Review, The New Republic, Ploughshares, Poetry Magazine, Poetry Miscellany, Poetry Northwest, Poetry Now, Prairie Schooner, The Seattle Review, The Sewanee Review, The Southern Review, Tendril Magazine, The Virginia Quarterly.* Special thanks to *The American Scholar* for awarding the 1982 Mary Elinor Smith Poetry Prize to "Prayer for Prayer."

This book is dedicated in friendship and gratitude to
PAUL MARIANI,
and with special thanks for advice and encouragement to
John Elder, Robert Houston, Gary Margolis,
and Stanley Bates.

CONTENTS

FACES IN A SINGLE TREE

❧ Early and Late

I hear the phoebe; she's returned to her
same nest this year. Are you awake? I hear
the mountain ash tree shudder with its load
of honey bees – I feel it, and I smell
crab apple blossoms lifting on the wind;
they must be opening. Throughout the night,
perhaps the soft vibrating of the stars –
something kept startling me, as if I had
good news to tell you, but I can't think what
it is. We've lived together fifty years,
our lives are what they were. How long is it
since we've made love? – there, now at last it's said,
it's openly between us, though we've shared
the knowledge every time we've almost touched.
Like fifty years ago, before we first
made love, old age makes you forbidden now –
as if it were some potion we had drunk.
     I picture you on Grandpa's farm, sitting
beside a stream, watching the maple leaves,
yellow and red, riding the blazing foam.
My brother, with a sailboat on a string,
played on the other shore, and so I paused,
uncertain – *should I try to kiss you now?*
A sweat-drop blew across your cheek and left
a hieroglyph as if on sun-warmed stone.
I must have held the kiss too long, because
you drew back. "No, not now," your breathing whispered.
On the first night you nursed Paul at home,
I watched the lamp behind you make a line
of hazy light to shape your silhouette.
I'd never seen your features quite so still;
you looked like Grandma on her cameo.
I laid my head upon your arm; "Not now,"
you said, "I don't think it will snow tonight."
I didn't ask if "Not now" was a sentence
meant for me, or for the coming snow.
     Last night you called out in your sleep, and then
I dreamed you visited my mother's house;

you both were standing at the open door,
she in a purple, flowered dress, and you
in white with noon sun reddening your hair.
You argued, though I couldn't hear the words;
she blocked your way from getting in the house.
I watched, and from the attic window where
I knelt upon a box, thinking I was
a child, I saw my hands upon the sill,
swollen with old, blue veins. A man came out,
with no shirt on, palms covering his face,
his skin white where the fingertips pressed in,
his shadowed muscles flowing down his arms;
you took his hand and started off with him.
"Don't go," I shouted, "Please don't go!" He turned,
lowered his hands, and gazed back in the house.
The young man there – that's who I was, that's who
you left me for! He paused once more, and then
you walked together down a pathway toward
a windless lake, diminishing within
an arching row of willow trees. We're told
that's how we see the farthest galaxies,
receding almost at the speed of light,
and vanishing except for their "red shift."
So what we know is only where they've left from
empty millions of light-years ago:
a shift toward red in the prism's spectrum
of a telescope to prophesy the past.

   News of the past arriving in the night:
your hair in sunlight and your silhouette;
the phoebe's whistle, and the thick odor
of blossoms opening; wet wind settling
and merging with the soft hiss of the snow;
everything held still in the mind at once,
everything here, and lost, and being lost,
equally unfolding, equally gone.
The autumn berries of the ash tree glimmer
still orange in the January snow,

at nightfall, shifting into red; I see
them now. Before the cedar waxwings left,
they could not eat them all; some are still here,
shrunken and brown, still clinging to the tree.
And you are here, and what we were – is here;
news of the past, I smell it in the dawn.
I feel that if I tried to love you now,
I'd gather in your breath, and hold it in
my own, and speak red words, and find a way.

❧ Making Her Will

Since Tom was born, I've never flown with you;
if we crash now, my brother and his wife
should be the children's guardians. She cares –
her table always has a bowl of fruit;
the pans above her stove make a design
of rising circles like the sun at dawn.
And when Stan built the wall around their house
with stones that he and Donny gathered from
the river bed, he would call "Now!" and *swoosh,*
from Donny's hands to his, the stone would slide
in place as if the mortared wall had willed
itself. I watched them work before you said
you wanted children of your own; your voice
was so deliberate you frightened me.

How could you let your sister raise our boys?
Painting is what she loves – in her queer way:
her morning valley mists are purple; even
her pines and hemlocks have a purple hue;
her still-lifes have no peaches, only plums
and shadows of more plums. Don't laugh as if
I mean this merely as a joke! Your sister
has a purple soul; she thinks she'll live
forever in some paradise of angels
lounging in their purple clouds. And if
she can't face death, how can she raise a child?
Paintings may last, but they don't live or die,
and even so, for how long? Everything
returns into the dark. My father's gone;
mother is ill; maybe our plane will crash;
maybe this summer at the waterfall
a child will drown just as your brother did.
A dead child is more loss than any mind
can hold: like mountains hazing into dusk;
like purple dusk dissolving into night.

Don't watch me from the corners of your eyes.
That's what your sister does. Her portrait of you
caught the rigid way you tilt your head –
as if your brother's voice called from beyond

4

the painting's edge. White tinted hair, she put
her white gloves on and stood there with her hand
poised in the surgical, fluorescent light,
glaring at her canvas till your lips
emerged an oily wet, with purple curves.
And then, for ornament, she made those curves
again, sketching your eyebrows and your ears.
Those curves were what she cared about – they made
her smile! I saw it sweep across her face!
I swear, if heaven is just, she'll have to scrub
the angels' underwear a hundred years
before her penance is complete. For what?
For purple curves – not loving life enough
to grieve we circle back into the dark.
    Your sister paints in order to forget
that nothing lasts; because your brother died,
she can't stay faithful to a living man.
How can she raise a child? You *are* like her;
your brother's death is still locked up in you
as if you could decide to keep him there
alive by holding back against your grief.
Did you *decide* to fall in love with me?
Maybe your sorrow did, to free itself;
you need my tears to weep your own. I see
the mountain, you, our gentle, handsome boys –
everything I love – hazing into dusk.
I see it – it's all there almost as if
it has already happened. I'm afraid
to fly with you today; I want my will
to be a circle with the words: I CARE.
    I've got to win this argument because –
because my brother and his son together
built a wall around their house; because
my brother's wife keeps peaches in a bowl!
You could decide, my love, and willingly
so that you'll be a model for our sons,
to let *my* passion have *its* purple way.

5

✐ Inheritance

    I'm worried that you want to go in debt
to me, buying yourself a partnership
in Arthur's firm. It's only two years since
you've earned your architect's degree. I know
he is your friend, but friendship's not engraved
in blood, and your assurance that you'll pay
me back . . . well, sons can't pay their fathers back
unless they give the same love to their sons,
and on until some final reckoning.
But what I care about is now – you're home;
it's been three winters since we've split some wood
together as we used to do, and there
are red pines I've transplanted from the field
I want to show to you. Just yesterday
a ruffed grouse crashed against the window and
mother decided it would make the right
Thanksgiving meal for your return. "It's like
the sacrificial ram, caught in the brush,
God gave to Abraham for Sarah's sake,"
was what she said. I let that pass; you know
what weight your mother likes to lay on things.
    The last year you were home she got so damn
possessive that I found myself competing
for your love. And then I felt left out.
She has a stronger hold on you than I.
Some day you'll feel your own life flowing in
your son, and then your debt will be redeemed.
One cool October afternoon, when he
is splitting wood with you, and you
are resting on a stump beside the sumac
blazing in the last warmth of the sun,
he'll take his T-shirt off, and as the axe
descends, you'll watch his shoulder muscles flex
and then release beneath his flawless skin.
A waterfall, you'll flow out of yourself,
and what you are will find its form returned –
as if the wind blew leaves back to the trees.

6

Don't be embarrassed that I tell you this;
it hurts for me to fumble with the words,
but it hurts happily, and that's the best
I have to give. Since you've been gone, I've planted
blight-resistant raspberries, too much
for us to use, but mother says she'll send
you her preserves. It has been hard, without
your help, to get the apples sprayed. We hope
you'll find a place where you can work nearby.
Arthur would not approve of that. I doubt
he understands what homes are for; he left
his father's firm to start his own. That's why
your mother takes the grouse to be a sign
to cherish your return, and why she made me
spray the raspberries all summer long.

We've got another hour before it's dark;
let's split more wood. The farmer's almanac
predicts sub-zero cold again this year.
The planet's changed. My father warned me: "Son,
the reckoning will come. Earth is our home
or else our grave." Those were his words. It was
a day like this, and we were raking leaves
still dazzling in their reds and golds. I stood
before him, naked to the waist, sweating,
thinking of your mother, trying to decide
what I would say when I proposed to her.

❧ Ghost Story

I've found three people now who claim they've seen
the girl's ghost underneath the apple tree
where she last met her lover on the night
he strangled her. Sue is upset with me:
she says things need repair around the house;
a grown man shouldn't waste his time asking
about ghosts. You know, Mom, that I don't believe
in ghosts, but she's become a legend here;
her murder gave the farmers something besides
planting to talk about. As you'd expect,
the girl was beautiful – with straight, black hair
that caught the moonlight like a summer lake;
astonished, dark-brown eyes; and skin so pale
some people wondered if she might be ill.
But no one could describe the boy, except
he lisped. The girl was pregnant when she died,
and everyone is sure he murdered her,
although he disappeared from town without
a fingerprint to make it certain he
was *there* that night. Her being pregnant doesn't
seem to me sufficient proof, and yet
it's also said the boy refused to help
his father with the milking chores. Three nights
I hid behind the old, stone orchard wall
to watch the apple tree, not expecting
truly to see her ghost, yet trying to
imagine her actually as she stood
there waiting for her lover to appear.
The third night someone came – a man, I'd say
about my height and build, and carrying
a stick or rifle, maybe hunting for
raccoons; or else her sleepless father might
have wandered through the orchard wishing to
out-walk his grief. I called to him. At first,
as if expecting me, he looked around,
then ran across the orchard to the woods.
Sue says I'm lucky that he didn't shoot.

Sue doesn't know I've come to talk to you.
The difference between Dad's books and what
the farmers saw is only that Dad knows
his characters exist as words. Explain
to Sue all *his* inventions are just ghosts!
And yet I wanted Sue to understand
the real fear that girl felt. Picture her face! –
that's what I should have said – surely someone
might have perceived the danger she was in,
and tried to rescue her. That's what her father
should have done – or else some neighbor's boy
who loved her, though she had rejected him.
And if I write her history, at least
her memory will live – if not her child.
    I'll get the details right – the scudding clouds,
the apple trees in rows, a piled stone wall,
the lacy, sleeveless dress that showed her arms.
But whom should I include – her father, Sue,
both you and Dad, a neighbor's boy, myself?
Sue's almost got to see her underneath
the apple tree in August moonlight, fear
on her hushed face, the shaded flowing
of her silver arms, a cameo around
her thin, tense throat, maybe just like the one
you always wear, engraved with circling whales,
that has my tinted portrait tucked inside.

9

❦ Coincidence

     Don't be alarmed! Let me sit here with you
to watch the waterfall. It may sound like
I'm telling you a tale, but listen, please,
then maybe you'll believe that I'm sincere,
and this coincidence, finding you here
beside this rocky pool, leaning against
this ancient tree with evening light reflecting
off the water on your face as if
you were the image of the waterfall,
may have some special meaning for us both.
  I met a girl, a year ago, sitting
where you sit now, her chin upon one knee,
like a statue, arms wrapped around her legs.
I told her she reminded me of someone
I once loved who died within her sleep.
She let me talk and liked my company,
and seemed to understand my grief as if
it were her own. I could have sworn her eyes
were moist when speckled light reflected on them
from the waterfall. She lived at home
out by the bay, but worked not far from me,
and she agreed to meet for lunch next week
by the stone lion at the library.
  I waited angry for an hour, fearing
someone had pushed her on the subway tracks.
Maybe she got the date wrong; maybe she too
had waited, felt abandoned, and gone home?
How could I know? And then I realized
I wasn't certain that I knew her name.
Laurel, had she said Laurel? I wasn't sure.
Could Laurel be her last name? What had I
to go on otherwise? And so I called
the Laurels listed in the Bayside phone book –
five every night. The tenth try that I made
brought me her voice in a subdued "Hello"
that seemed to echo from some distant cave.
One second I was sure, but then she said:

"There's no Miss Laurel here." I realized,
abashed, I knew the voice – I must have called
my mother's house. Pretending innocence,
I said "Excuse me, please," and left the phone,
wondering if she knew that it was me.
    Having run out of Laurels, I then tried
some other names of other plants or flowers,
randomly selected, for I figured
coincidence was now my only hope.
And yet I always asked "Is Laurel home?"
One night a voice replied "Miss Laurel died
over a year ago." I hung up trembling,
never made another call. But then
I dreamed Laurel sat by the pond where first
I saw her just as you sit now. Slowly,
as if floating step by nearing step
along the mossy path, I reached to touch her
when she turned to me and raised her arms.
Her eyes and mouth were blurred – as if reflected
upon water, moving as the water moved,
murmuring, but not with words. A lion
resting on a rock, guarding his high cave,
nodded: *if I returned I'd find you here*.
    I knew I'd see the pond-light on your face;
I knew the waterfall along the stones
would echo human sounds – calling sounds
and pleasure sounds. I'm sure I've seen that lion's
look of sorrow on your face before.
Can you believe me though you may suspect
I've read this story somewhere in a book?
While this light lasts, maybe you'll let me touch
your lips, and then you'll tell me who *you* are.

❧ Persuasion

You want to marry Jane – my daughter Jane?
For God's sake, Bill, you and Nancy drove me
to the hospital when she was born!
You said that I was blessed to have a girl.
You've been my closest friend for twenty years!
Each New Year's day till Nancy died, you helped
Jane dress her snowman in your ear-muff hat;
you would confide to it through your cupped gloves:
"Now you don't have to listen to the wind!"
   The camping trip we took that spring before
Nancy had her stroke, when Jane slipped crossing
a stream and sprained her knee; you lifted her
up on your shoulders, but she cried for me
to carry her. You sulked the whole way home
as Nancy teased you: "Every woodsman needs
a daughter of his own!" Her laugh cascaded
like a waterfall – until the stroke
twisted her eyes; her mouth drooped to a scowl.
I wondered if her illness angered you
and changed the way you treated her, although
you told me at her funeral you thought
you couldn't love again. A hailstorm tore
the apple skins the day she died – winter
in the blazing midst of summertime, I thought –
and I remember that you said: "At my age
friendship is enough reward for me."
   And now you want to marry Jane! I know
that friends can be replaced – that hurts, but not
what hurts the most; Jane's age hurts even more.
Did you know that my mother was in mourning
when we met on that canoeing trip?
You sat upon a boulder by the shore,
and as I landed my canoe, you put
a finger to your lips to quiet me
so you could hear the early loons reply
across the water where the wind had dropped.
The o͞o in loon brings back my father's voice,

mellow and distant, yet for all the times
we've listened to the loons call by a lake,
I never told you how my father died.
Though he was forty when he married her,
each anniversary they'd pack a tent
and climb Mount Marcy's steepest trail; I think
he died while they were making love. My sister
still resents his death and hasn't found
a man to marry yet. Spring love is for
putting in the seeds; summer is for tending;
fall is for gathering and letting go.
    It's not too cold yet, Bill. Let's spend a week
canoeing on the Allagash. We'll fish
and listen to the water lull the shore,
letting our voices drift across the lake
until we hear our echoes in the pines
sigh and fade out in the receding wind.
And you'll forget. Nancy would want you to.
I still can see her laugh at what she called
our "woodland ritual," her forehead veins
blue as a rivulet, her eyes just like
my father's – ice gray flecked with gold. The loons,
the soothing loons will help you to forget.

❧ Secrets

      I doubt that you remember her – except
that final summer when we took the house
beside the bay. I vowed to wait until
right now to tell you how your mother died.
Do you still have her photograph – the one
in which her hands are cupped, with you trying
to peek inside? Every morning even
before I woke, she took you for a walk
to search for starfish scattered on the beach.
You were excited after you returned,
but then you'd sink into a sudden gloom
without a cause that I could see; you'd go
into your room and sit there with your shells,
arranging them in boxes; you'd stay inside
all afternoon. At night your mother talked
about your moods, though in your room, I thought,
when playing with your shells, you seemed content.
    You had one smooth quartz stone, your favorite,
and every time we looked you had it placed
inside another box. A thousand times
your mother asked me what I thought that meant.
I thought the stone meant you; the boxes meant
your made-up lives. Your mother thought the stone
was her – that you were putting her away –
but never told you what she guessed. Claiming
they were all beautiful, especially
the rounded stone, you scared us when you said
it was the only one that had itself
inside itself. The way your mouth was fixed
warned us to inquire no more. Your mother
wept all night; we held each other, kissing
gently in the dark, though something private
deep in her sobbing tightened her. She said:
"I don't know why I haven't done things right."
    I promised her we'd take a trip, and when
her spirits rose, it seemed to me that you
no longer switched the stone from box to box.

14

We flew down to Bermuda where we took
a cabin by the beach. At night we strolled
the curving shore, collecting colored stones
and sea-shells to bring home, or curled together,
hugging, naming whatever stars we knew.
She told me things I'd never heard – like once
her mother ran off with her father's friend.
One moonlit evening we undressed each other
on the beach to take a swim. We raced
into the water, holding hands, and then
I let her go so I could watch. Flawless
as polished marble, oh her smooth arms gleamed,
plunging like dolphins as she dove; wind gusts
blew clouds across the moon, and she was gone.
    "Didn't you search for her?" the captain asked,
"Couldn't she swim?" "The water was so dark,"
I said, "and yes, she grew up by the sea."
"Was she depressed?" he asked, and I assured him
she was never happier. "Strange tides,"
I thought I heard him say. Sometimes I dream
that she gets washed up further down the beach,
having forgotten who she is and who
we are, and that she is alive, living
another life. And then I am awake,
wishing something familiar – like the feel
of stone – might bring us back to her. We must
forget the past; we have a new life now.
Alice loves you – she's all you really know
since she moved in with us. Can you recall
your clinging to her on our wedding day,
helping her unpack? You kept the picture
of her sitting on her mother's lap.
    I didn't tell you how your mother died
because so much remained unknown. Promise
never to tell Alice – she's heard enough.
This has to be *our* secret; promise me.
This little golden starfish – take it, Joan –

I've saved it for the necklace that I gave you
when you turned thirteen; your mother bought it
by herself the day before she died.
She said that having secrets was her way
of holding on, and that you'd understand.

❧ Piano

When Dick left on his trip last week, and I
moved in with you and Dad so you could help
while I was nursing Sue, I heard you play
for the first time, and learned Dad bought it as
a wedding gift. Why have you waited all
these years to play again? I don't mean to
invade your privacy, but a daughter
has a friend's right to show she cares. I've watched
your ritual of setting hyacinths
upon the piano-top before you play;
you breathe so deeply that it seems the notes
come back to you right from the flowers' scent.
Has my return affected you this way?
  But now I have a daughter of my own;
I also know what things a wife can't tell
her husband, not exactly things she's done,
but things she's thought. Though Dad loves music, still
he seems uneasy when you play; he pulls
his ear and puts a finger in his mouth.
I want to share with you, while Dick's away,
my mother-fear of being smothered by
the people I love most. How much do you
reveal to Dad? Have you suggested that
there may be ties between my coming home
and your piano playing after almost
thirty years? At Dick's goodbye, he stood there
in the windy, sunlit doorway; yellow
and red maple leaves swirled into the house
as if his parting were their chance to make
themselves at home. And then he handed me
the hyacinths. That night when I moved back
to spend this month with you, Dad said, "Their smell
gets stronger after they begin to droop."
  I didn't notice then that no one played;
the piano stood in its own space as if
the silence needed shape to hold the thoughts
we couldn't share. Before Dick left, he wanted

to describe his business friend in Rome:
"We're so alike, it's weird, but Phil's wife is
your opposite. Last visit, after she
had gone to bed, I read her diary;
'Dick is a warm, informal man,' she wrote,
'but somehow I don't trust him in my house.'"
Dick might have told that story either as
denial or confession; or it may
have been his hinting that he trusted *me*.
   I ought to understand why you're released
to play the piano now. Something I need
to know about myself is hidden there;
music must be your way of telling me.
I still suspect that Dad dislikes the scent
of hyacinths, although he used to read
me ancient tales before I went to sleep –
of Hyacinthus' blood that was transformed
into a purple flower by Apollo
who had killed his friend by accident.
But when Dad listens to you play, a frown
like yours creasing his face, and his fingers
keeping time or twitching on his stiff knee,
maybe he thinks of losses you and he
have shared – maybe my leaving home. Perhaps
it's not for me you're playing, but for him?

Brother to Brother

I bought these garden shears for you to help
me to explain the time I took Dad's shears
and told him I last saw them in your room.
I meant to borrow them to cut barbed wire –
I knew they weren't made for that – but when
I chipped the blade, I panicked and then threw
them in the pond. Dad's anger flustered you;
you stood there with your hand over your mouth,
though maybe you were laughing – I don't know.
    For years I've asked myself if this were worth
confessing; yet last night I dreamed your son
had found the shears while diving in the pond
for turtles, and again I felt the need
to ask for your forgiveness – just as when
I told your wife you used to make me sneak
into their room at night to see if they
were making love. Everyone fears the dark;
what's wrong is that I dwell on it too much.
Some common sight – like sprouting corn planted
in rows across the field to the wood's edge,
each shadow a hieroglyph upon the earth –
can make me cry out with the surging wish
to hold that scene forever in my mind.
You're so absorbed designing houses that
you don't have time to think how long we're dead.
    Maybe Dad's death disturbs me more than you
because I see myself in him, and when
he punished you, although I took his shears,
I guessed that you resented both of us.
He loved repairing things around the house,
but first he loved to prune his apple trees.
He'd eye a branch, his arm outstretched, holding
his breath until he knew exactly how
he wanted it, then snip as if its life
depended on it. "Light, it needs more light!"
he'd say to me, and snip again. And yet
to picture him alive reminds me that
he's dead – I just can't get my grief to end.

Sometimes I envy you. You seem to watch
yourself as if you were somebody else,
amused with what you see. But I still see
Dad's pruning shears, poised for another snip,
catching the light; the circle of moist wood
at the cut apple branch, catching the light.

❧ Sister to Brother

Look, there it is – I'm sure that is the oak
we built our tree-house in the final summer
Grandpa was alive. The tree-house that
you built might be more accurate; you never
let me hammer; passing nails was my job.
   Thanks for not asking why I brought you here;
maybe as my brother you can sense
what's troubling me. Those summers on the farm –
we were close then, with Grandma watching us:
'You've got to take your sister," she would say,
"a family is like a hand – fingers
are useless one by one." Sit here with me
beneath the oak, I want to try to talk.
   I haven't been myself – I'm pregnant and
I don't know if the father's John or Bill.
I thought I'd better wait to choose which one
to marry until I slept with both, and now,
whichever one I choose, it would be like
marrying two men; the other's ghost
would be there in my bed – and in my child.
   I'm thinking of not keeping it – it's still
only a little hungry speck of cells.
Should I discuss this with both John and Bill?
And what if one says "Yes," the other "No"?
Last week, when I had lunch with Dad, I felt
I'd lost hold of myself. He was about
to pay the bill when suddenly he looked
much younger than he's looked in years – his face
seemed smooth, his nose more aquiline, like yours,
his lips more curved and tilting to the left.
And then I thought: "My God, what if he's not
my father after all?" Now do you see? –
I've lost my sense of what it's safe to trust.
   It's crazy, but the hardest thing for me
to talk about is that I feel it's you
who are to blame for this. Remember how
you made me bait your hooks when we hiked down

to fish in Grandpa's pond for perch and bass?
They'd wriggle to get free; how could they know
that it was not my fault? I still can't stand
the taste of fish, the crumbly meat. Sometimes
I'd sneak off to the tree-house by myself
and make believe you'd gone off on a trip;
I wrote the letters that you sent to me.
Then Grandpa left and died away from home,
and Grandma wouldn't talk of him. She'd weave
until the window light would fade, and say:
"This is the best work that I've ever done."
    How did you get her tapestry from Dad?
Dad always claimed that it belonged to him.
But Grandma liked to weave things in for us:
I'm sure that tall oak in the woods behind
the farmhouse is our tree, and those white specks,
like trickled light among the rounded leaves,
maybe they're you and me. You should have told me
Grandpa left to die; he was afraid
we'd see him broken at the end. And yet
what I suspected was much worse. Always
something's missing that I need to know.
    After the farm was sold, you didn't seem
to care for me as much, or notice me,
and it's been years since I've asked for your help.
After my lunch with Dad, that whirling night,
still feeling that I couldn't trust myself
and therefore couldn't keep the child, I dreamed
I pulled a baby out of Grandpa's pond;
it had your face. It stood up, waved goodbye,
and walked away into the yellow house
of Grandma's tapestry. Maybe the reason
I can't decide is that I never knew
whether you *had* to love me – was it me? –
or was it love for Grandma's sake? That's what
I mean, there's always something I don't know!
    What difference can it make to you to know
who my child's father is? I'm sure, if you

adopted it, Grandma's ghost would say:
"I'll weave it into my next tapestry;
a family must hold together like
a hand." Then I could try to start again.
Just ask your wife, I know she'll understand;
some women can't have children of their own.

Heather, three years have passed since you've been here
with me, and it was raining that day too –
so hard it sounded like the leaves were seaweed
slushing with crumbled shells against the shore.
I'm sorry I insisted that you come;
I know you need to get away with Dave
before your baby's due – your father hoped
he'd have a grandson since there's only you
and Beth – and yet I felt you ought to see
what someone's chiseled on the back side of
your father's stone. I'm not sure who it is,
although before your father died, he had
a client, Ben, a taciturn young man,
accused of bludgeoning his brother in
a drunken fight, but he convinced the jury
Ben was not the kind of man who murders
what he loves. Your father spoke with such
persuasive eloquence, I never won
an argument with him. He'd wink when I
gave up a point because he understood
I'd do exactly what I had to do.
    Ben turned to sculpting when he was released;
perhaps he feels he's paying off a debt
by etching on the stone. See, there it is –
it must have taken months: the animals
in pairs, the ark beneath the risen sun,
with Noah and his wife waving goodbye,
though not one beast turns back for a last glimpse
of where it's been. Look at the care that's gone
into the etching of the lion's mane,
the knotted shag around the camel's ears!
Only the dog is there without its mate.
Could Ben have wanted it that way? Perhaps
there wasn't time for him to finish it.
    Beth comes here by herself; she likes to be
alone with her own thoughts. She was the one
who first discovered that the stone was marked.

I never looked behind it when I placed
a cedar wreath upon his grave because
he didn't like cut flowers, though he knew
their names: bloodroot and toadshade, adder's tongue
and wet-dog trillium and spiderwort;
he would recite them like a witch's chant
to make believe he had me in a spell.
Beth worries me. The quickness of your father's
death still troubles her. The birds she paints
have such large eyes that look directly at you
from whatever branch or stump they're on.
I wonder what Beth thinks they see in us.
The dove, she says, should not be carrying
an olive leaf; that's why the carver left
his work undone. Heather, it bothers her,
I'm sure, that you got married first, though she
is four years older than you are, and soon
you'll have a child. Beth hoards too many feelings
for herself – or for her staring birds;
she holds grief back so it will never end.
    Did you know Audubon, meticulous
observer though he was, painted some birds
that no one else ever has seen – as if
he'd really watched them perching in the woods?
People need ways of making things their own.
Your father kept a life-list of wild flowers:
Heather was underlined – I noticed that,
cleaning his desk after he died, and I
imagined how he chose that name for you,
walking along the dunes beside the rocks.
    I'll tell you what I think. I think that Beth
is seeing Ben, that she instructed him
to make engravings on the stone. Ben didn't
realize that flying *from* the ark
the dove would not have held an olive leaf,
so Beth decided that he stop his work.
And I suspect . . . Heather, don't give me that

aggrieved, exasperated look of yours –
as if you think I've planned all this to get
you here to mourn your father as you should!

❧ Spaces

Dad, you can work the Skil-saw while we talk,
then let me have my turn to finish up.
I need to borrow money. My old friend,
Teddy, offered me the chance to buy
into his firm, designing private homes.
Be careful, watch the blade! I've talked to Mom;
she loves the house Teddy built for his Dad —
the picture windows and the cave-like rooms,
so that close space flows outward to the field
and gathers where the willows frame the lake.
  A house should be an image of the mind —
it should invoke the feelings people need
that don't exist until there is a form
to hold them in. Mom said you might not let
me pay you back; I know that in the deepest sense,
I can't, but something I can pass along
I've learned from you will grace each house I'll build:
of balances, of lines repeating and
of forces that connect. Mom says she's saved
some money just for me; she thought it might
be easier if I used her money so
I'd feel that I was starting on my own.
  Mom said her mother left it all in trust
to use when the time came. I must have been
about thirteen when Grandpa cut those oaks
to use as barn-beams; Grandma hardly talked
to him for days. "They'll all grow back," he said,
but Grandma told me that he could have bought
them somewhere else. I think I understood
how people love things in their different ways.
Pausing to sniff the wood, Grandpa whittled
at it like a sculptor; he'd close his eyes
and rock his head as if in prayer or drunk.
  Maybe I could borrow half the money
from you and half from Mom. But Dad, you've got
to let me pay you back. If you insist,
put it in trust and save it for my son.

27

You're always getting wood-chips in your eyes.
You rest, I'll work the saw a while . . . I said
let me measure the next few boards. Teddy
has a commission for a house right now
he wants me to design – it's just my kind
of landscape with a view along a row
of pines and cedars leading to a lake.
I told Mom that I'd like to have the roof
slope upward from the west to east; I want
a feeling of the flow of space outward
past trees and lake and, if the night is clear,
into the constellations of the stars.
    You're going to hurt yourself today! I'll cut
those last few boards while you clean up.
I shouldn't give away my strategy,
but Mom suggested that I talk to you
while you were sawing wood. I've never kept
secrets from you; I know you see through me
too easily. There goes that grin of yours;
you're worse than me at keeping feelings in.
Promise that you'll let me pay you back.
I'd like to build a house for you someday,
but you won't move from here. We both know that,
though Teddy told me that his parents felt
the same way once, and I'll admit, Mom guessed
I could persuade you if I timed it right
with all the scented wood-dust in the air.
    That grin of yours is more suspicious than
I thought at first. Tell me the truth, come on,
where did Mom get the money? It's my hunch
you figured that I'd be either stubborn,
like knots that break the rhythm of the grain,
or too proud and refuse to ask for it.
I think she may have gotten it from you.

Trying to Separate

Please give me room, Howard! I've tried before
to tell you this – I have to leave you, oh
that came out wrong, there's no way I can find
the words that sound as if I'm making sense.
Not *you*, Howard, it isn't *you* I'm leaving,
it's Vermont, the starving deer, the spring
that never comes, the gloomy ice and clay.
Even when late sun lingers in the birches,
darkness fills my mind. I need more light,
more red – not just a pair of cardinals,
but flocks of them. There's no red in the earth;
purple spreads in the mountains when the sun
descends behind the hemlock trees as if
the animals were grieving there. And fall
comes much too soon, the yellows are too brief;
I don't have time here to forget myself.

I want to go to Tucson where I lived
before my mother died, where stones are red,
the desert light *feels* red – a gradual,
slow, steady red. I need more time to dwell
on images I want to paint. Don't joke
again about my always *seeing red!*
You once said that my painting is the cause,
but that's not first; I need a different light
than you to *see*, and then the paintings come.
You need Vermont, you need an inward light;
you need the feeling that each day is hard.

Love cannot feed itself with love. We've tried.
Love needs something outside itself – children –
and we've delayed deciding that too long.
You said one only chooses children after
one has had them; then they become like *place*,
then they're the *given* like the landscape is.
You think there's got to be some deeper cause
for breaking up. I fear you may be right,
but I can't find that cause; Howard, believe me,
I've really looked. All that I know is red,

and you desire gray; punishing winter
is your season, white birches are your light.
You need Vermont to be yourself. You do!
    Don't try to comfort me; don't touch me now —
that makes me angry when I want to talk —
for then you'll have a reason I should stay.
You'll say: admit it's *me* you want to leave,
admit you're angry, that it's not because
you love the goddamn red; you'll say we have our sunsets
blazing on the snow, we have our fire at night,
as if I'll give in like I always do.

❧ Nursing and Dreaming

Why must you nurse him in the living room?
Waking alone in bed confuses me;
I think I'm dreaming or I'm somewhere else.
You have been gone over an hour, dozing
in my old chair. The fire is almost out;
the groaning down-draft makes it smoky here.
I'll warm some milk for you, then come to bed!
He'll sleep unless the dead elm's cracking branches
startle him. Or did I dream that too
with mother standing at the open door,
my brother in her arms, her smooth white legs
shining with their own light? I heard the rain
behind her and the creaking trees as if
someone – the wind? – were following her there.
    Again tonight I woke and couldn't tell
the baby's wailing from the wind. I switched
the lion's-head lamp on by the bed; it yawned,
and then I saw my father's silence in
its opal eyes. Drink up your milk before
it's cold! I want to finish the same dream
that started when our son was born – about
my brother coming home – the night I saw
you staring through the down-pour at the elm
as if you'd nursed here in another life;
I promised you I'd take it down to stop
the wind from blowing branches on the house.
    Can't you nurse him in bed so I don't have
to ramble through the house in search of you?
I used to sleep-walk when I was a child.
His cries wake me up anyway, or else
I hear the door-latch click no matter how
you try to close it quietly. There's something
you don't want to say, and yet I sense
I'm dreaming what you wish for me to dream.
    Your body's changed, your breasts, but I can't tell
my unchanged body how to wait for your
return. I'm no one in my dream or I'm

not me. My father's death must be the elm,
although that figure past the door reminds
me of my father too – unless he is
the both of us combined, just as my brother's
also my son. And since you don't appear
as my own wife, I feel I've lost you and
myself, though here you are, nursing our child,
with real wind clacking branches in the elm
and drizzle misting in the garden rocks.
　　Finish your milk – then let's go back to bed;
tomorrow, if the wind is still, I'll cut
the dead elm down and bury the remaining stump.

❧ At the Terminal

I have to change planes here, but I'm afraid
to fly again. We hit a down-draft over
the Rockies, plunging us a thousand feet
before we leveled out. Everyone screamed –
as if we had one voice that followed us
to testify what happened at the end.
All I could think was that we must be falling
faster than the speed of sound – *nothing*
about myself was in my mind. Death seemed
impersonal; I didn't feel embarrassed
when I wet my dress. The reason I
sat here by you with all these empty seats,
is I mistook you for Mom's doctor who
delivered me and cared for us since I
was born. The likeness is remarkable,
although you're younger by at least ten years:
you have his sapphire eyes, his bony hands.

My ears throb like a fish washed on the beach;
I'll cover them when the next plane takes off –
or else I'll hear that scream. See what I mean?
Only a smoky wind was in my mind,
as if I'd never lived my life, as if
my father never said "We'll miss you" when
we kissed goodbye. There should have been pictures
with golden frames so I could think the times
I watched the sunrise with my brother from
our tree-house by the lake, hearing *plink* sounds
of leaping perch – plucked strings of a guitar;
or past my bed-hour, with Mom scolding him,
Dad led me to the "hooting grove" where owls
called out across the restless dark, responding
to their echoes or their mates. We'd try
to pick the call that started the replies,
but never could be sure. There always seemed
to be a first before the first we heard.

"That's 'concourse wild of jocund din' for you!"
Dad would exclaim. I still can hear his voice

exactly, for I knew his words were not
meant to be understood. I should have thought
of them beneath the scream – Dad's moonlit teeth,
and wooing owl calls pleading in the night
their soothing, melancholy sound. My mind
was empty as the plane plunged down, and now
I feel I'm listening to someone else –
maybe it's mother's voice – talking to you,
although your stare tells *me* I'm beautiful.

    Mom said that all men fall in love with women
they have rescued, since men suffer from
some barrenness themselves they need to cure.
I think you're thinking that you'd like to spend
the night with me, and that I'd whisper little
owl songs in your ear, reminding you
of someone you once loved. These hollow noises
dizzy me – these voices gathering
with each departing plane. Why do they call
such places terminals? Nothing ends here!

    We're only passing through. I see your wife
waiting for you at home: she's peeling apples
in the sink as gold flecks on their skins recall
your eyes. She turns the faucet on and hears
the distant voice of someone she might marry
if your plane should crash, blushes, and then
returns to who she is, the naked apple
shining in her hand, not knowing that
beneath the long, pursuing scream, your last
framed picture was me talking to you here.

Dear Seymour Penn

FOR PAUL CUBETA

For thirty years my wife and I have read
your books and wondered what you're like. Before
she married me, during the war, she loved
a man who has your name. He disappeared,
and all these years I've thought that you might be
the man she knew. Her photograph of him
looks like your last book-jacket pose, but he
was so much younger then, I can't be sure.
The picture is enclosed; you'll be amused,
for there he is – laughing, leaning against
a redwood gate beside a lemon grove,
his feathered hat in hand, and gesturing
for everybody to come in as if
to smell the ocean in the lemon trees.
   My wife has been too shy to write herself,
and anyhow you know how women like
to fantasize; that's why I've always let
the matter pass. But when, in your last book,
I read a passage where a man like me –
unknown, mindful of others, getting old –
exactly in this circumstance, decides
to write and ask an author he admires:
"And have you ever loved my wife?" I felt
finally it was time to contact you.
   I hope to learn if you're the man who knew
my wife, but since the author in your book
chooses not to reply – although it's clear
he has the aching need for reaching out –
I have no clues. So I've composed a scene
in which the author, fascinated by
the picture sent him by a man like me,
writes back to say: "Astonishing though it
may seem, the orchard keeper by the gate
could be my brother, lost at sea after
he bought a lemon grove; he planned to bring
his would-be wife out to the coast so they

could settle there." A sign above the gate
reads: SOUR IS SWEET, I guess, because the first
two words are cropped. The picture makes him wish
he'd lived the life his brother might have lived –
each pungent day among the lemon trees –
and he decides he wants to write a book
about a couple married thirty years.
A bachelor, he makes a strange request;
he asks if he can visit us to learn.
"You'll hardly know I'm there," he promises,
but I can sense he sees my wife through his
lost brother's eyes; already he is half
in love with her, staring at the pulse-beat
that startles like a sparrow in her neck.

And that's the story's gist so far. But if
you want to know what happens next, then I
can send you more; even you, a master
plot-maker, will find yourself surprised.
I trust this bond of ours because I feel
us touching as I write – as palpably
as sunlight shimmering the lemon trees.
Beneath the blandness of most people's lives,
incredible things occur – like now, like this.
These thirty years – they are all frozen there
across a wall and through a redwood gate.

In my own life, I've waited for your book
to tell me what to do. And now you have.
You knew the author in your book could not
explain himself, that I would have to write
his history. When I knew what you knew,
I smelled the ocean in the lemon trees
so powerfully, the salt stung on my lips.

My wife sends her regards, and wonders if
you would believe her lover is my own
invention, that the picture here enclosed is me.

◑ Painter to Self-Portrait

With quick, repeating lines, pine needles bristle
into sight; a greenish smudge becomes
the trees' scent of voluptuous shade. Across
the valley, purple covers blue, the self-same colors
shadowing your eyes as you sit, watching
from a rock, the taste of blueberries
still on your lips. A northern, gray wind blusters
through with sliding shades, reminding you
your wife has gone to live with someone else –
his thick jaw, his uneven ears! Perhaps
the same wind darkened in the firs the time
your mother left your father for a man
who lived in Tucson, saddened in a week
because it didn't rain, and she returned.

His portrait of her shows her naked, pale
to the waist, folding her arms beneath her breasts
to lift their circles to the rubbing light,
between two giant saguaros, both in bloom.
As if reflected on a lake, a coyote
curls within the throbbing cactus shade;
a silhouetted figure, halfway towards
the mountains maybe twenty miles away,
stares above the ragged tree-line at
the orange rock. Her diary may have
combined two stories since, before your birth,
your father left a desert girl to join
your mother who was waiting in Vermont.
He painted her in soft, receding snow-light
beside a waterfall descending from
the painting's edge, her hat pulled to her eyes,
remembering a former lover's hands.

Perhaps you'll find, within the blues emerging
from the mountain mist, the reason why
your mother left him as he rested, gazing
by the window, where a nuthatch pecked
an icicle, recalling how the wind
wove through the August aspen leaves, flashing

their undersides, and scared the nesting grouse.
The first night she was gone, after her flight,
the swelling sun released its heat, making
the desert mountains bronze; her lips were dry;
they hurt her when she kissed him hard until
her body drew her into sleep. Your mother
never called him by his name, though she
described the golden fleckings of his eyes.
"The fear of loss," she wrote, "becomes a space
we fill with fantasies, a windy space
that separates our lives from where we live:
the lizard on his stone, his throat puffed out;
the leaping doe across a sloping field."
    Just like your mother, your wife will return.
As fox cubs bark beside their den, I'll set
the mountain range at dusk in darkest blues
and place your children in the windy woods
beside the waterfall; it will be March,
and she is walking at the field's north edge –
a stone wall piled a hundred years ago –
calling to them, "Come home!" too far away
to see your face, too far away to know
who waits for her upon a purple rock,
if it is you or just some trick of light.

❧ Dear Sally Rivers

One life is not enough – or so it seems
with Hank, though we've been married twenty years.
I still can see him by the picket fence
his father made him paint each spring. "Hey there,
I have an extra brush, give me a hand!"
were his first words to me. He didn't seem
to notice that my hand was not quite right.
Not that he's been unfaithful; I believe
his shocked assurances are true. But he
admires your husband's novels so darn much,
his people (as Hank calls them) are so real
to Hank, that when he talks of them (a lot!)
I feel as if they're living in our house.
   Last night when I complained (I rarely do),
we argued half the night, and then I dreamed
I gave birth to a girl – your husband's child.
Today I broke a pitcher in the sink –
my mother's wedding gift – and I resolved
that I would write to you. We live almost
secluded by a lake surrounded with
old willow trees. I like my privacy;
most of my day is spent in tying quilts.
I am designing one right now with geese
migrating past a hazy sun, stroking
their wings in unison, each one assigned
to its own place. I'll send a photograph
when it's complete, and if it pleases you –
tell me your birthday. Virgo is my guess.
   In his last book, your husband's heroine
is crippled in an accident; only
her daughter goes on loving her. I wonder
if she's modeled after you. If so,
perhaps you'd like me to explain (I'll try)
how I have dealt with *my* infirmity.
Just let me blurt this out: your husband has
made people from some need to feel complete;
how can you tell that you're not one of them?

How can you tell you're not invented too?
Hank needs me as a listener. He talks
about your husband's characters as if
they were his own, and gives them lives that change
the book: "If Jack had left Corinne . . ." and off
he goes where I have no desire to go.
    I feel I've never been alone with Hank.
(I've never caught him looking at my hand.)
He says I'm like our lake at dawn before
the wind's first stirring in the willow trees –
as if that were his final compliment.
My mother thinks that Hank's best feature is
his smile, and yet his cuspids are so large
they press against his upper lip. Maybe
this will amuse you: when I married him,
I dreamed I stole back to the picket fence
to paint the outermost two pickets black.
Hank's told this story now so many times,
he's come to think my dream is his. "Without
those teeth of mine," he'll say, "you never would
have married me; you would have married Bill."
And off he goes with me just listening.
    Men are like children in their needs. Did you
applaud your husband when his book was done? –
"Bravo! my darling, yes it's beautiful!"
Even if true (as in your husband's case),
there's something human such truth fails to touch.
    Before I send this letter off, I'll take
another walk around the lake to watch
the trees' reflections as the colors change:
the lake absorbs the blue-grays of the sky
and passes on a purple hue to tinge
the yellow willow leaves. (One can mistake
a cedar waxwing for a robin in
this light.) Then I'll be ready to decide
whether to sign this with a pseudonym.

☙ At the Ecology Convention

Don't you remember me? It must have been
almost ten years ago – salmon fishing,
the Ryans' cabin up in Maine – that we
slept together. What are you doing here?
I'd heard you and your husband moved out west.
Your hair was darker then, you wore it straight,
and when you swam it covered up your face –
except your nose. You would pretend you had
to find your way back to the shore by smell.
    Those red curls fooled me when I saw you here,
your grayish eyes seemed rounder, but noses
reveal one's inner self more than eyes do;
babies' noses all look the same. Have I
embarrassed you? I didn't mean to talk
so loud. You knew we'd meet again; before
you fell asleep that night, you mumbled through
your sighs, like my first wife, "We need . . . we will."
The windy rain swirled right across the lake,
tore the boat loose, then suddenly it fell
so softly we could hear each hollow note
like bird calls underneath the eaves, and sniff
the odor wafting from the cedar woods.
You lay so still, your face framed in your arms,
repeating rain sounds with each breath, and then
you cried out in a moan: "Have you come back?"
I couldn't tell if you called in your dream
or if you were pretending that you slept.
    The Ryans have split up. I tried to buy
the cabin from him, but he sold it to
a logging firm. At first I guessed he left
to be with you. I hardly knew her, yet
she wrote to me to say that *she* left *him*.
    Her letter seemed to have a cedar smell;
I wished it came from you. Maybe you've heard
I've taken on the pseudonym, "Cedar,"
just that one word. You know, the human brain
distinguishes among six basic odors:

putrid, fragrant, spicy, burnt, ethereal
and resinous. Hunger, humidity,
a woman's cycle of the month, and fear,
sharpen the sense of smell; migrating fish,
locating the first stream they swam by smell,
return where they were spawned; bees entering
a foreign hive are killed because the wrong,
betraying scent of their clan clings to them;
a female moth in heat attracts more than
a hundred males in half a day; if she
released the whole supply of bombykol
contained inside her sack in just one spray –
which she would never do – a million males
would gather to her in a single hour.
　　Tonight I lecture here on moths. We are
all creatures, everything we do is willed
by what our species signals us to do –
even making believe. Before I sleep,
I sniff the forest in the cedar branch
I keep under the lamp beside my bed,
and then I dream I'm on that shell-strewn shore,
watching as you approach, pushing your way
out of the weedy lake, brushing hair from
your lips to ask who called you back. You see,
I understand why you pretend my name
has slipped your mind; you need to know me deeper
than my name can say. You must have smelled
the cedar twig, pressed in this book my wife
willed to me when she had to go away.

∽ The Cracked Apple Tree

      Right on that branch we saw the snowy owl
the one time it arrived from Canada.
Don't cut it down! I know it's past the age
for bearing useful fruit; it crowds the house
and darkens both the upstairs rooms, but we
have changed the place enough – the well is new,
the paneled walls, and all those shelves you built
are crammed with books. The day we bought the house
old Phillip put it in your mind to clear
the trees that blocked the vista to the west:
"People like to fix things up themselves,"
was what he said, and yet we've left it there
for over twenty years, just as you've left
his broken harrow rusting in the field
as if it were a piece of sculpture, though
it's like the rib cage of a dinosaur.
      Phillip was *afraid* to cut it down;
he told me that he saw a girl's ghost there
whose lover murdered her when she got pregnant.
She lived down the road before this house
replaced the one that burned, and Phillip said
that we can find a record of her death
somewhere in the local files. Last week
when you were pruning it, you left your sweater
hanging on a branch, and when I took my walk
beside the stream before I went to bed,
I saw it flutter in the moonlit breeze
and thought of Phillip's story of the girl.
      My father kept a bear's head in his den
over his desk: he teased me as a child,
pretending that the bear would talk to him.
I never found out if he shot the bear.
      I know you like to watch that great stone ridge,
framed by the distant Adirondack range,
after the brittle leaves have fallen down.
I've seen you sit beside the window, staring
at the long striations – yellow, tan, and brown

turning to orange as the sun comes up –
as if you saw something you couldn't share.
I've warned the children not to bother you
when you take on that inward mood of yours.
    What if a blizzard drives the snowy owl
down here again, and he can't find his branch?
What if the man returns, filled with remorse,
seeking his lover by our apple tree?
One can't be certain such things don't occur.
Your books are full of mysteries and puzzles,
half-invented memories, and choices
that can't be explained. You'll never know for sure
if Phillip made the murder story up
about the pregnant girl as an excuse
to leave the tree uncut. You'll never know
if I invented father's talking bear.
I saw the look that crossed your face when I
told you about the girl; I'm certain you
were ready then to let me have my way.
    You leave the harrow lying in the field;
you keep your thoughts about the layered ridge
and what its colored lines remind you of,
and let me keep the cracking apple tree
for our love's sake. For if you don't, my dear,
I'll put my wedding nightgown on and stand
there in the moonlight on the tree-stump, still
as your ridge, as if I were a snowy owl.

Trying to Reconcile

You shouldn't have gone off the pill without
your telling me! Even if we decide
to have the child now, even if it's mine,
it was your choice, so don't pretend your motive
was to help the marriage last. A prick
groping the dark for some anonymous
relief, that's all you wanted me to be,
that's all I am. If you believe a child
can bind our lives, allow me time to come
to feel that for myself. But it's control
you want – another way I'll need you and
you've got me then! I want a child to free
something in me more generous than sex
that brings me back to my own emptiness.
I've got to reach you, and I've got to try
to try, or else I'm only me again.

Maybe we've lived in this same house too long.
I see the same striations in the cliffs
emerging orange from the mist each dawn.
The short-eared owl – I've seen him sitting like
a glacier in the moonlit apple tree
a hundred times, the same ancestral grip
still holding him, the mouse limp in his beak,
always the victim with his testament
of blood upon the snow in March, and yet
without regret like you and me, breathing
our remorseful sleep, blaming each other
for what we lack ourselves. Maybe we need
enemies to injure, more loves to betray,
to learn those cosmic patterns of defeat –
like limestone fossils in our hearth. I could
read pity there if we asked less of love
to rescue us from being what we are.

Watching the stars, pity is what I feel
for all of us, gaping with thoughts of leaving
our own lives, banished even from ourselves
like stars receding with their reddened speed.

Will they come hurtling back, explode, and start
the whole damned thing again? I'll rant my way
back to *my* life – at least that's better than
accusing you of my own emptiness.
　　It eases me to watch the whipping snow
piling against the trees to starve the deer
who die without a plea in their white minds
for help to come. "Hidden death" you called the pill,
"refusing to accept we'll be replaced."
It's like my fantasy of strangling you –
as if to take a life could save my own.
　　Look there by the gully – it's the lame fox
whose broken leg we set last summer when
he was abandoned as a cub, staring
at us with his black eyes. Is there a chance
that he remembers us? "An empty casket
where a life should be," those were your words
that made me *taste* the pill. I'm listening,
trying to feel your thoughts as if I touched
my own, as if your choice were in my groin.
　　"Someone's got to help that wounded fox,"
you said, "since its own mother won't." "That's not
the way that Nature works," was my reply;
"now she's forgotten it's alive." You know
I'll love the child. You know I know it's mine,
don't you? I have no choice except to choose –
choose something or we're all just whirling stars,
just snow the blind wind heaps upon the snow.

❧ Going and Staying

The first time that your mother flew to see
her father when he had a stroke, I dreamed
she almost crashed, and when she flew again,
the dream returned. I watched her climb the stairs,
then turn and wave. Her lips called "Stay in touch!"
although she couldn't spot me in the crowd;
and then I saw her calves, her purple shoes,
the sun's glare on a wing as if it were
a windless bay, and then the dark inside.

A white-haired man with outstretched geese embroidered
on his tie — whose face I couldn't quite
make out — sat next to her, and when the dark
blinked smoky red, he drew her to his chest.
A wing exploded, pivoting the plane;
I woke before it hit the ground, angry
at her, and asked her not to fly that day.
If there's a wish contained in such a dream,
my son, it's not the wish I chose to wish.

That night we held each other, and the fear
drained from my body, but I dreamed again —
again she climbed the windy stairs, the sun
gleamed on a wing, the old man's blue-veined hands
fondled her sunken head. The burning plane
spun earthward as his features changed — his lips
grew redder till he was a child; I woke
when his flushed face squeezed to an infant's cry.

Still half asleep at breakfast, I could see
wild geese migrating through the surging mist;
I pleaded that she wait another day.
But when she left this house we built together
and the apple orchard that we tended with
the drunken bees, I saw her silent lips
say "Stay in touch!" as if somehow she knew
when she arrived, her father would be dead.

Look how the mist recedes! One cannot tell
exactly where the snow-capped mountains end
and where the clouds begin; even the pines
seem shadows that the clouds cast on the wind.

I haven't had that dream again, but when
I hear the misted geese, those images
return — red darkness, and the man, grown back
into a child, touching her cheek. After
her father's funeral, when she came home,
I thought you noticed that we did not kiss.
You said you'd never want to fly. And yet
it's beautiful up there — distance does that,
and I'm afraid loss does that too. The wheat,
the harrowed earth, the tassled, gleaming corn,
seem painted only for the color's sake.
But if I dream tonight, maybe I'll see her
flying to visit you, her final "Stay
in touch!" before she died, parting her lips.
She'll gaze outside to hear the apple blossoms
humming with the bees and watch the colors
of the landscape stream away below —
as if those words were meant for everyone.

ᕍ Disappearance

FOR DAVID AND PAMELA HADAS

I can't believe you don't remember whether
Grandma's eyes were brown like Jill's or gray
like mine! Dark gray – I'm almost certain, Mom,
that they were gray, set close against her nose.
You've always said I have her stubborn way
of seeing people as I wanted them,
while Jill was more remote and critical.
    Doesn't it scare you, Grandma's only dead
three years, and she's begun to blur. I see
her shuffling in the kitchen, never outside
in the sun, stirring her pot of stew,
sipping the spoon, with steam around her ears
as if she conjured her own autumn mist.
My clearest memory: she's scolding you –
her tightened hair in its eternal bun,
her breasts puffed out like some endangered bird
that's summoning its brood – because you failed
to telephone Aunt Jenny on her birthday
as you promised Grandma that you would.
"Sisters have got to keep in touch," she said,
"no matter how your lives lead you apart."
    You were offended by how Jenny dressed;
I heard you tell Dad that you didn't want
her in the house with her cheap rabbit fur
and her array of phony mink and fox,
but she would mimic you when she dropped by
and make Dad laugh so hard he'd snort and grunt.
I hated Dad's crude laughter; I was happy
Jenny moved away when Grandma died,
but I regret now I once felt that way.
    Before she disappeared, Jenny arrived
to talk to me, just me. I'd never seen
her wear so many furs: her hat, her coat,
her gloves, even her boots, and I almost
didn't recognize her with her eyebrows
penciled in black, her lips slicked shiny white,

49

talking so rapidly that little foam balls
bubbled at the corners of her mouth.
She frightened me, holding my wrists to make
me look directly in her face as she
informed me Grandma loved you more than her.
She spoke those words in broken whispers, then
she tugged her hat and told me I was more
like her than you, and that I mustn't feel
dishonest when I disapprove of you.
  I don't know what connects these things, but when
you said you weren't sure if Grandma's eyes
were gray, Jenny's long face came back as if
a fox poked from its lair and stared at me
across the hillside through the windy snow.
Was Grandma as composed as she appeared?
I never heard her shout or saw her rush –
or has your memory lost hold there too?
I just can't see how you forgot that your
own mother's eyes were gray! You'd better look
at me as carefully as Jenny looked.
  I'm good at hiding what I feel, that's why
I half suspect Jenny wore furs to show
we all need some disguise, providing that
we don't disguise ourselves too perfectly.
She never told you where she went, although
I'll bet that she left Dad her number just
in case. . . . She'll know if Grandma's eyes were gray!
If we forget one single hair of hers,
everything else from toe to fingertip
will follow down the light and slip away
like Jenny walking off that afternoon
into the shaded snow. She saw me watching
from the window when she doffed her hat
and laughed as her black hair came slipping out.
Her eyes were gray like Grandma's, and like mine,
and maybe that's why you forgot, or why
you're wondering if Jill knows that I'm here.

Ask Dad, I bought this hat for you only
because it's been a cold and windy fall;
I had no premonition that we'd talk
of Jenny after all this time, so don't
assume there's meaning in my choosing this
birthday gift – it's coincidence – except
that I remembered and I care. Dad helped
select this beaver hat, it's genuine,
because he knew Jill couldn't come today.
Jill didn't tell *me* why she couldn't come.

✑ Cleaning the Fish

Mom says she won't; we'll have to clean them, though
she used to do it when I fished with Dad.
Dad's illness wore her down; I think she felt
relief after he died, and didn't mourn
him long enough before she married Sam.
   I know there is an art to cleaning fish.
In ancient times, prophets could look into
the future by examining the entrails
of an animal; they'd burn it then
to satisfy their chosen deity.
   Hold down the tail, and use a scraping knife,
stroking the scales to get right to the skin.
Slice through the vent and open up the fish,
just like a box. Then pluck the organs out:
liver, bladder, stomach and gills; cut off
the head and tail, and wash away the blood.
This tissue here – this iridescent film
that runs along the whole backbone – must be
removed with care. How smooth the small heart is!
It will continue beating for a while.
   Fish don't feel pain like people do; they go
right into shock without the fear of death,
like other animals, because they have
no thought of time extending after them.
They don't know what loss is; you mustn't feel
sorry for them. Don't be upset with Mom.
It was because of us that she remarried
so soon following Dad's death. She knew
we needed money and a healthy father
in the house after those draining years.
   When Sam bought you that dress with yellow birds
you've wanted for a year, you hardly said
a word of thanks. But I predict that he'll
be kind to you and Mom. I've told him how
Dad sang to you before you went to bed,
even when he had lost the melody,
until the very end. Sam understands
the way the dead still live within our minds.

The clearest memory I have of Dad –
he's pasting in his stamps, studying them
with his magnifying glass, looking for
the special marks that make them valuable.
The ones he loved the most were animals,
bright red and blue, I think from Africa.
He told me that he never traded those.
I saved his whole collection for a while,
but then I had to sell it to a friend.
  Enough of that! Today we concentrate
on fish! First, rinse it in cold water, dry,
then lightly rub with salt, inside and out.
A shallow dish is what we use, and top
with sherry, soy, and peanut oil. Later,
I'll give you all the measurements. Sprinkle
with parsley, garnish with some shredded scallions,
and, behold, a two pound fish should steam
for twenty minutes and be done! Take out
Mom's crystal glasses, Grandma's silverware,
the yellow tablecloth, and light the candles
when the sun goes down; they shine with orange
merging into purple blue, almost like
the inside of the fish. When you grow up
and marry someone whom you really love,
you'll teach your daughter how to clean a fish.
  If Dad were still with us, he'd show approval
with his eyes: "Life must serve life," they'd say,
"here's to good food!" And Sam, well we'll find out
whether he has an appetite for fish!

❧ Sister to Sister

You've shared too much to leave Jim now. Is it
another man? I've paid the price for searching
for a perfect love, as mother warned.
Remember how she loved to put things by?
Each jar was packed with still another bean
or cucumber; she'd say: "There's always room
for just one more." There always was. I still
can picture her preserves: blueberry jam,
strawberry jam, raspberry, cherry, quince,
tomato sauces, jar after steaming jar,
the tiny seeds sparkling like yellow stars
in their red galaxy. She placed the jars
in open shelves where everyone could see,
row after row, in greens, in blues, in shades
of red and orange. "That's my rainbow,"
she would say, "I'm Mrs. Noah, maybe
you've heard of me." Living alone, what can
you prove by that? We all need someone's help.
    Can you repair your plumbing, wire your stove?
Accepting help from strangers can't protect
you from the need for love. I've learned to live
with emptiness, watching the sea, and that's
my strength, though I can fill the morning hours
when I write with characters invented
for my book. I make them suffer as I
weep for them. Like you, one leaves her husband;
she regrets it only later when her
daughter does the same. After her father's
sudden death, she visits her old mother
to tell her that she's met a novelist,
fallen in love, and wants to live with him.
Her mother is preserving fruit. She warns
her daughter: married love is what a lifetime
must embrace, especially shared sorrow.
Holding an empty jar, framed by the window
where evening sun streams through in dusty beams,
she says she loved her husband to the end

when all those plums and peaches, luminous
in their juices, labeled in her print
to give their dates, lined her kitchen shelves.
   Don't leave Jim for another man; please read
my book, you'll see! I think some parts are funny –
like when mother, Mrs. Noah in the book,
decides to breed angora rabbits, but
every one turns out to be a girl.
The pet store owner I made up remarks
there's little difference for the naked eye
to see, and Mrs. Noah falls in love
and sleeps with him, just once, right in the store
with all the puppies yelping in their pens.
The last scene, which I still may change, will show
the daughter's daughter, preserving blueberries,
wondering if any happy ending
can be true. We all need something, even
if it's sorrow, to survive ourselves.
   But you're my sister! You know if you have
to leave him, if you really must, for just
a little while, you could move in with me.

✎ *Trillium*

Maybe I shouldn't tell you this – you are
his daughter, Beth, as much as you are mine –
I think your father's having an affair.
Last spring he started hiking in the woods,
just as he used to do when you were born;
he said he needed time to be alone.
But then I noticed he began to mention
subtle things about the flowers – details.
"Everything about the trillium comes
in threes," he said, "petals, sepals, stigmas;
the ovate leaves, all three of them, whorl right
below the triple shining crimson flowers."
He'd follow me around the house, describing
what he'd seen, and get annoyed with me
if I did not respond enough. Last week
I couldn't help myself; I blurted out:
"What *do* you want to say to me?" I see
you're skeptical, and yet you know your father
well enough to sense when he is holding
something back. Why should the fact a flower
has suggestive names – like wake-robin,
stinking benjamin, wet-dog trillium –
be so significant to him, unless
there's a confession in those names, hiding
even from himself? He says wake-robin
is its name because it blossoms just as
spring arrives. I think he feels that spring
can come again for him. At our age, Beth,
men often have the need to start again,
and you'd be wrong to think your father's not
like other men. You love the wilderness
and gardening; you know the wild flowers' names
and when to plant the lettuce and the peas.
Why can't he take you sometimes on his walks?
   I figured you'd get angry if I spoke
what's really on my mind. Lately you have
so little patience when I try to share

my thoughts with you — as if our being close
threatens your sense of who you are. I'm sure
you know that stinking benjamin describes
the odor of the trillium — it's like
a sweating body, a body dying
or making love is what he didn't say.
I'm asking only for your empathy,
not condemnation of his so-called walks.
No daughter ever loved herself unless
she loved her mother also. Beth, I'm scared,
I don't know how to meet this need of his,
and I'm too old to start again — not old,
but old enough to want to keep the loves
I've built upon: his love, my dear, and yours.
And his remaining here gives both of us
the needed distance it's so good to cross.

　　Remember how the two of us would bake
his birthday cake? I'd let you split the eggs,
and you'd sit on the kitchen counter, spreading
thick brown fudge in swirls, touching my lips
with one delicious finger. You believe
all this is fantasy — that father's walks
are innocent? What has he said to you?
I think you're keeping something to yourself.

　　When you were in my womb, you'd press your head
against the pulsing of my artery.
You were the hardest child to get to bed,
and when from sheer exhaustion you let go,
your lips would tighten and expose your teeth,
your mouth turn downward with a little drool;
I'd stand there looking, baffled by such sleep.

　　Is there a chance he'll leave me for this *girl*?
What do you think? We haven't talked like this
in years — about the birds and flowers, no less!
We make a funny triangle: husband,
wife, and trillium — till trillium do
us part. Thanks for the smile — I need it now,

and promise not to ask what else you know
about my rival, wet-dog trillium.

Ferns by the Waterfall

I knew you'd marry again. Mom's been dead
two years, and I'm prepared. She'd sit there on
that ledge beside the pool; she loved to read
while savoring an orange or a pear
as I was catching tadpoles like a boy,
searching for salamanders under logs.
I always had to call her twice before
she'd hear and lift her head up from her book –
as if she wasn't quite sure where we were.
Janet has hiked back here with me; she's seen
the pool swirling below the waterfall.
She took her clothes off once and dove right in.
   Don't feel obliged to ask if it's all right
with me for you to marry – you're still young,
you have your needs; no one should live alone
or die alone. If you love Janet, marry her,
she can decide whether your doctoring
will leave you time for her. What troubles me
is how Mom died. Why did she go alone
to swim at night so late in September
under the waterfall? She never went
there by herself before. When she got home,
shivering to the bone, she woke me up
to ask if I would rub her back and arms;
I couldn't break out of my dream in which
somebody – maybe you – was strangling her,
and I still have the strangest feeling that
the dream repeated something I once saw.
I'll wake at night, thinking I hear her moan,
and then I see you in the hospital,
your stethescope around your neck like some
great spider hanging from its threads, saying:
"We doubt there is a link between the chill
and what shock later caused her heart to stop."
   Soon I'll be leaving home, I'm seventeen;
there's more I need to know. Why did I dream
of someone strangling mother on the night

she stole off to my waterfall? Climbing
a ridge, trying to escape from someone,
she called out, but no words would come, only
slobbering sounds. And as I woke, wanting
to help her with the words, just as he reached
her throat and covered her, I dove into
the pool, and heard those sounds on my own lips.
I still feel I'm stuttering when we talk.
    Had I seen Janet before mother died?
She's not like Mom at all; she'd rather hike
than read or listen to a symphony;
she knows the names of ferns: elk's horn, hare's foot,
and maidenhair. I can't imagine how
you met, and yet it seems I know her from
another life. I saw her watching me
when we were naked at the pool. "Look how
the light reflecting from the water makes
the birch limbs dance"; then coming close she gazed
at me, a long, slow gaze: "Bird's nest," she said
as if her list was now complete. Mother
also loved ferns, but not out in the wild;
her flowers were arranged, circled by ferns,
yellow balancing blue, and with a touch
of purple or red. Nature, for her taste,
didn't make the right designs, squandering
its precious colors unwatched in the woods.
    I've needed us to sit beside the pool,
listening to the waterfall, before
you marry Janet; and I'll pick some ferns
for us to eat tonight. Before she had
the killing stroke, we were alone, and Mom
asked in the hospital: "The ferns, I need
to know all of their names." April's the time
when they begin uncurling into fronds;
now that they're tender, they're called fiddleheads.

✒ Incurable

I recommend the oysters here! Savoring
good food helps slow me down and pace my thoughts.
 Maybe I've had a prejudice against
surgeons since my mother's operation,
but I believe you're trained not to respond
to suffering; that's why I disapprove
of Margaret's marrying you. I'm sure you think
I'm not prepared to let my daughter go,
but I'm convinced surgeons are trained to learn
how not to grieve. Look at you now – there's not
a ripple on your face to show you don't
like what I've said. You're taught to think of flesh
by feeling with a knife – as if the line
dividing cruelty from cure were drawn
so fine, only a steady hand, and not
the blundering, brave heart, could trust itself.
 I brought you here, this meal's on me, so have
the sirloin steak, the mushroom sauce is done
exactly right. After my mother's stroke,
they cut the left side of her neck to clear
the blocked-up artery and get more blood
into her brain. I watched for one whole week;
her speech returned, she could remember me.
But then another blood-clot formed; her chin
drooped to her chest, she drooled, baby sound "$\overline{oo}$"s
bubbled upon her tongue. The surgeon said
"We'll go in on the right" as if there were
some hidden life reserved inside her head
that he alone could find. He had the look
your eyes have now when he said "Operate!
We'll try to save her life." What life is it
if she can't think? – humiliation of
poor flesh, gasping its dumb dependency!
 You cut her open and her soul flew out,
leaving a limp creation, an impostor.
I watch you lift your glass, and I can see
my daughter in your hands, numbering

her ribs beneath the skin, naming the organs:
liver, colon, lungs and spleen. How could
your fingers know if *she* is lying there?
Touching like that's no cure for loneliness –
that's why I left my wife, and why I want
my daughter cherished more than hands can do.
　　When Margaret was thirteen, we visited
the lake we lived by when she was a child.
Explaining why I had abandoned home,
I said "Mother and I have fallen out
of touch." We don't touch when our bodies touch
was what I couldn't bring myself to say.
She hugged me as the spindrift loon-calls spread
across the water with the evening mist;
then she pulled back. Softly as possible,
I put my arm around her as we walked,
and yet my love could not reach far enough
inside where love gets recognized as love.
　　Then there was nothing I could do except
protect her from my own possessiveness,
and now I must protect her happiness
from you. Maybe I'm wrong, so here's a test
to prove you too can honor suffering:
doctors have professional ways of easing
people out of pain. Release my mother
from the dungeon of her bones; give me a pill
to rescue her. Margaret need never know;
I won't breathe one small sound of what we've said,
but I'll know that you're capable of love.
You'll have a father's blessing if you do.

෴ The Homecoming

You need to know I knew that John was ill;
I never meant to keep this to myself.
Although we hoped to reach Maine before dark,
the farm my father sold some twenty years ago
was only fifteen miles off our route,
and John turned off the highway as I asked.
It's time, I thought, to tell him why we had
to leave the farm. He sulked a little as
I stroked his finger with the silver scar
just like a ring; he felt we had delayed
this holiday too long. When we arrived,
a cold gust swung the cedar gate; John laughed:
"Your mother's ghost is welcoming you back."

The house was only used in summer time;
it was locked now, although a lantern burned
over the entry door and from the upstairs
where my bedroom was, to warn off hunters
now that hunting season had begun.
I looked inside; a hat hung on a chair
resembling the plaid cap my father wore.
Behind the house a row of apple trees
had gone unpruned and wild for all these years;
our tree-house in the oak had lost one side.

A tense red squirrel watched us as we crunched
along the path to find the spring-fed pond
we stocked with bass. Though shrunken now, more slime
along the edge, its border willow-stand
composed a golden web against the sky.
On Casting Rock my brother got a fishhook
wedged in his palm; I still can see his hand –
the swelled, blue spots where both barbs entered in.

Talking to you now, trying to decide
if we're right for each other, I recall
John bent behind the boulder, scraping mud
from his grooved boots, but watching me. Even
without turning my head, I sensed he watched.
I stared at dry leaves thrashing in the pond,

then closed my eyes. "We owned a mare," I said,
"who nuzzled her foal and licked its nose and ears,"
and John, as if he read my mind, exclaimed:
"We have our own child now. It's time to go!"
He pulled my glove off, gripped my whitened hand,
and tried to lead me briskly past the house;
the door-lock must have sprung as it used to
when sudden wind blasts speared down from the north.
"Let's look around, just quickly," I implored.
    The red hat on the chair was not my father's,
yet I could picture his flushed ears, flaming
as if his blood had angered in his veins
when he returned from hunting in the dusk.
We went into the kitchen where we found
opened soup cans – just as rifle shots cracked
across the hill. We wondered if strangers had
broken in or had the legal owners
hunted there? I felt John must be told,
and I commanded "Follow me!" in tones
I'd never heard in my own throat before.
    Steep as I remembered, we climbed the stairs
to where my parents slept. "It happened there,"
my low voice murmured. "They were arguing.
Their shouting woke us. We crouched beside the door
clutching each other. Mother glared at him,
then cupped her hand over the candle flame
as if to catch the light, as if to hold
and keep some needed warmth. And father stared.
I heard flesh sizzle. I can smell it still,
and I can hear her scream circling the room
around my head. Then somehow I was somewhere
far away; and now I'm here with you,
trying to tell you so I can forget."
"You should have told me long ago," John said;
"I'm not sure now I can believe it's true."
    The hunters had returned with a huge buck
strapped to their jeep; its long tongue slipped across

its jaw, and its cut belly steamed as if
the dead heart's final heat might warm the air.
John told them why we came, and led me back
as snowflakes wavered in the slate-blue dusk.
John died before he could be sure; I woke
beside him but he was already cold.
    My son needs me; perhaps that's warmth enough
for any woman. I won't blame you if
you think it's wise for us to wait a while.

❧ Leviathan

FOR JOHN AND MARY ELLEN BERTOLINI

You've kept your word and come to visit me.
You know how much I love this house, although
I'm lonely here. Your father used to walk
this beach with me, then sit on that smoothed rock –
as if the sea prepared a seat for him –
observing sails tack past the buoy bells,
waiting for a whale's spout to appear.
It seemed he would forget how many times
he told me: when he was a boy, he took
his row-boat out to get a close look at
the baby whale that strayed into the bay.
Descending underneath your father's boat,
it surged up bubbling on the other side,
flipped around, dove beneath his boat again,
drenching your father with each salty plunge.
Circling beyond the reef, its parents flung
their thirty tons into the sky – with a
vast whoosh of blown-out sea, their plume of spray,
and then a hiss of air as if it sucked
the whole horizon in – displaying white
repeating patterns on their undersides,
pounding their tails to summon its return.
Your father claimed it dove beneath his boat
at least a dozen times before it left,
but he regretted that he didn't leap
into the sea himself to play with it.
I'm still amazed to think how all his life
that rankled him, and yet that may have been
the most ecstatic day he ever spent.
"I swear the damn thing laughed at me," he'd say,
"its whistles, chirps and clicks composed a song."
     Your father thought he was a happy man,
but something willed about his happiness
showed through, something deliberate. I felt
he had to make a choice to hold gloom down.
And yet he couldn't bring himself to say

66

what troubled him; I don't know if he knew,
and never did find out. A certain blank,
distracted gaze would sweep across his face
when that grim mood of his came on, making
his eyes seem vague – the way a camera
blurs one's age-lines when it's not in focus.
Sadness in him – if it is accurate
even to say that it was *his* – rarely
connected with particular events;
it simply would emerge and disappear
like hemlocks in the autumn morning mist,
and there was nothing I could do to help.
I had to live with it, so I assumed
that I was not the cause. Last night you spoke
to me in that remote, abstracted voice
your father sometimes used, when you remarked:
"There's just one man my wife would leave me for –
our son; it's like competing with a ghost."

   Your father used to praise me for the care
I'd given you and Jennifer, but not
the caring I showed him. I don't mean he
would blame me for his sorrow, yet I'm sure
he wished somehow I could have found a way
to lighten what he called the tears of things.
How could I? What he felt was much too deep
and too impersonal – like rain, or mist,
or snowfall in the oak's remaining leaves.
I fear he passed that sorrow on to you.
Yes, he was right about himself – sorrow
revealed the soul of things, especially
when they were beautiful; sorrow for him
was out there moving in the universe.

   Perhaps he loved the changes of the fall
too much: the orange maples, goldenrod
at the field's edge, and you, your muscled arms
just like his own. Before you left, you split
the last dry cord of wood for him. He leaned

against the window watching you, and when
you came inside – do you recall? – he told
his story of the baby humpback whale,
but with a change. I'd never heard before
that when the whales dive down and disappear,
they leave patches of oily water, almost
imperceptible and strangely still,
which look like human footprints on the sea.

❧ Remains

My ship departs next Saturday. Ruth knows
I have to go. This time, Dad, keep in touch.
We'll study whales, both stranded and alive:
their great intelligence, how they maintain
communication over distances
with sonic pictures showing what they feel
from sounds produced – they have no vocal cords –
within their lungs. Think of it, Dad, pictures
of what they feel from sequences of clicks!
Their brains are larger than a man's; the links
connecting stimuli to response are
inexhaustible; their memories possess
a power we can barely comprehend.
Professor Singer says they demonstrate
a vast capacity to show affection.
　　Tell Mom that Ruth and I have broken up;
I'll write to her. Mom warned me once that Ruth
could not accept my love because Ruth feels
she isn't worthy to be loved. And now
I'm not sure what remains to be explained.
Ruth kept accusing me – though it's not true –
of loving someone else, and yet perhaps
I did hold something back. She'd say: "All you
talk about is whales." But we're killing them!
A hundred tons of pain with each harpoon!
Millions of years evolved what Cousteau calls
"extraordinary gentleness." No whale
will hurt a diver if he's not attacked,
and yet we're killing them! The great blue whale's
almost extinct. I can't accept a future
with no whales remaining in the sea,
but Ruth won't get involved, although she knows
what sorrow is. And if I write to Mom
to say I've got to help the whales, she'll think
that's *my* excuse for leaving Ruth. Not so.
Our species can't embrace our mortal lives,
and killing makes us feel omnipotent.

The twenty-pound harpoon grenade explodes
inside their flesh. Reports describe their cry –
part howl, part plea; they dive down, opening
the hooks which gouge their organs out. They're dragged
back bobbing to the ship. The sea swirls red;
the air takes on a fiery haze. You know
the whale is dead when its gigantic mouth
opens as if it were about to speak.
A whale will swim between an injured whale
and the harpooning ship; or if he's hurt
and has become a burden to the herd,
he may decide to stop his breath and die.
It's difficult for whales to mate because
they're too huge to plunge in like simians;
there's pain in their repeated, strained attempts.
Whales breathe like us, so they must rise and sink
together as they try to merge, using
their flippers to embrace each other's bulk.
Often the sea clouds with defeated sperm.
Gray whales require a second male to help,
to lie across the coupling pair so they
can keep their balance in the churning sea.
Ruth wonders how they've managed to survive
through the millenia. Mom thinks such mating
shows they are incapable of love.
    You've got to hear the whales sing, hundreds
with modulating voices: mewings, trills,
janglings and whoops, creakings and bellowings,
each making its own sounds for the sheer joy
of making sounds. Lagorio remarked
"It's a cathedral in the sea!" We can't
explain those alternating calls, unless
they're joining with the family of whales.
    When I left Ruth, I pictured you and Mom,
still young, in your first house, and lost myself
thinking that I was you, imagining
you could foresee you'd have *me* as your son.

The swaying bed became a whale, holding
me there, more buoyant than I'd ever felt,
and all the whales were singing, praising me.

I know it's not the first time you've been stung.
I know it hurt; the swelling closed your eye.
When I was stung I threw up from the shock.
But I can't sell our hives. Sweetheart, caring
for our bees, raising them with Jim's help, makes
me *feel* the seasons turn. If I believed
in God, "I'll tilt the planet" would be His
initial words. Jim's almost old enough
to tend the hives himself; he has your cool,
maternal touch. When he removes our honey
from the hive, the swarming bees stay calm –
as if they trusted him. When honey bees
are shipped, the queen bee is protected in
her own small wooden box, surrounded by
thousands of worker bees. If she were not
secluded in her cage, the other bees
would kill her, since the odor she emits
would overwhelm them. So a sugar cube,
about a pencil's width, is fitted in
a hole on one side of her cage. After
we shake the bees into their hive – I've let
Jim handle them for years – the boxed-in queen
is lowered down to them. The time they take
to eat the cube and thus release the queen
into the colony, allows them to
adjust themselves to her so she can move
toward darkness at the bottom of the hive
where she will lay her eggs. The colony
is like a tree – a *single* living thing
with separate parts: roots, trunk, flowers, leaves.
   The worker bees collect the food – like leaves
from sunlit air; the queen, like roots and trunk,
connects one generation to the next;
born in the spring, drones resemble flowers
in their brief flourishing. The queen retains
their genitals after they mate and die;
death is no tragedy to them. Their lives

continue in the colony as if
their whole philosophy might read: "The bees
that follow me are who I am." When Jim
and I last gathered honey from the hive,
the sweetness so excited him that he
forgot he wore his black protecting veil
and wildly threw his arms around my neck.

I'll tell you something bees can't do; they can't
pretend. Imagine you are me, wishing
to will your son a gift just like the trust
a nursing infant's body learns upon
his mother's breast. Think of *me* feeling that!
For him the morning light is still blue shadows
hazing into purple shades; besides
his mother's breath, he hears the knocking of
a bee against a window where a vase
contains a sprig of cherry blooms. Sweetness
is what we need – sweetness passed on to be
remembered by. Ask Jim how *he* would feel
if you insist we give the hives away!

After two years, when the fatigued queen bee's
fertility diminishes, she is
deposed by worker bees. But that's where all
analogies collapse. We need to make
believe that human love has lasting seasons
of its own – as we once vowed to do.

Don't try to pluck the stinger out! Some honey
smeared upon the swollen flesh will help
as well as any remedy I know.

ce Prayer for Prayer

Darling, splitting the wood can wait until
the wind dies down. I want to try to say
what's troubling me, although we vowed before
we married that we'd keep our own beliefs
and let the children choose. They've left home now;
there's not much more that we can do for them;
it's you and me together, only us,
and I'm afraid you won't get into heaven,
not having turned to God. Without you, how
could I be happy there, unless God wills
that I forget this life? I don't want that!
The March sun hasn't thawed those icicles
gleaming along the edges of our roof;
perhaps this constant wind has numbed my faith.
  I've never had to ask you this before,
but would you try to pray? Make up the words
if only for my sake; start thanking God
for daily things like breakfast oranges
heaped in the yellow bowl your mother painted –
a couple bathing in a waterfall –
our wedding gift of thirty years ago;
thank Him for your routine: feeding the birds
in winter, pruning apple trees in spring;
thank Him for splitting wood. You know I know
that even when you grumble, still it's work
you love. Nothing I do will feel complete
until I've given thanks for doing it,
so that I'm not alone: like thanking you
for thanking me when I prepare a meal
adds grace to grace. That's not a phrase you'd use;
you would prefer to hold some meanings back:
"Grace is not fattening, how can it hurt?"
but what we feel is not so far apart,
though maybe it's the very space God wants
to test us with? My mother used to say:
"You cannot cling to what you love with all
your strength; God made some special part of us
for letting go." I understood her when

74

our children left, and I can almost hear
the spaces where they were. Maybe sorrow
is allowed in heaven, so God won't have to
cancel human love by making us forget?
    I won't forget, not willingly; one day
in paradise, watching the clouds, I'd think
of you standing beside the frozen stream,
eyeing the wood still to be split and stacked,
and I'd be back on earth – at least at heart.
God means for marriages to end with death,
but after that the Bible isn't clear.
Perhaps God's love begins where human love
completes itself, and yet I'll never tire
of the past we've shared. I know you'll promise me
you'll try to pray, and then you'll ask the Lord
to help me find the strength to give up prayer –
as if God would enjoy your joke; you'll swear:
"By yonder icicle, I'll love the world until
it does me in!" Thinking is the problem;
we can't escape the sorrow of an end
without an end, death going on and on.
Although you never speak of it, I know
your father died while he was splitting wood;
your mother's telling always starts the same:
"Some snow had fallen on his knitted hat . . ."
as if for her all time had stopped. Maybe
that is what heaven's like? She seems to smile,
but then the age-lines darken in her face.
    Darling, I know you know something in me
approves your laughing at my need to pray.
By yonder icicle, what human love
allows, we have! But don't stand grinning with
that orange in your mouth as if you were
some sacrificial pig! Go split more wood
while I put dinner on; listen to God's
silences even as the wind blows through
the icicles and piles snow by our shed;
we may be in for quite a night of it.

ROBERT PACK

has taught for twenty years at Middlebury College, where he is now Abernethy Professor of Literature and Director of the Bread Loaf Writers' Conference. His books of poetry include: *The Irony of Joy, A Stranger's Privilege, Guarded by Women, Home From the Cemetery, Nothing but Light, Keeping Watch,* and *Waking to My Name.* Pack lives with his wife and three children, among apple trees, in a valley by the Green Mountains in Cornwall, Vermont.

❧ FACES IN A SINGLE TREE ☙

was set in Galliard by DEKR Corporation, Woburn, Massachusetts. Introduced in 1978 by the Mergenthaler Linotype Company, Galliard is based on a type made by the sixteenth century's Robert Granjon, and is the first of its genre to be designed exclusively for phototypesetting. The name Galliard stems from Granjon's own term for an 8-point font he cut about 1570. It undoubtedly refers to the style of the face, for the galliard was a lively dance of the period.

    Galliard possesses the authentic sparkle that is lacking in the current Garamonds. It is a type of solid weight, which will bring good color to the printed page — an asset in offset printing, in which the more delicately constructed romans appear to disadvantage. The italic of Galliard is particularly felicitous and reaches back to the feeling of the chancery style, from which Claude Garamond in his complementary italic had departed.

The book was printed and bound by The Maple-Vail Book Manufacturing Group, Binghamton, New York.